JONATHAN HARVEY

Passion &
Resurrection

CHURCH OPERA IN
TWELVE SCENES

for soloists, chorus, brass, percussion, strings and organ
with optional audience participation

TEXTS OF BENEDICTINE LATIN CHURCH DRAMAS
TRANSLATED BY MICHAEL WADSWORTH

(1981)

Piano reduction by the composer

VOCAL SCORE

FABER *ff* MUSIC

Music and libretto © 1998 by Faber Music Ltd
This edition first published in 1998 by Faber Music Ltd
3 Queen Square London WC1N 3AU
Music processed by Donald Sheppard
Cover design by S & M Tucker
Cover illustrations from the Issenheim Altarpiece by Matthias Grunewald.
Details from *The Crucifixion* and *The Resurrection* © Musée d'Unterlinden, Colmar.
Photograph by Octave Zimmermann reproduced by permission
Printed in England by Hobbs the Printers Ltd
All rights reserved

ISBN 0 571 50616 X

To buy Faber Music publications or to find out about the full range of titles available
please contact your local retailer or Faber Music sales enquiries:

E-mail: sales@fabermusic.co.uk
Website: http://www.fabermusic.co.uk

Commissioned by Martin Neary with funds provided by the Arts Council of Great Britain. The first performance of *Passion and Resurrection* was given by the Waynflete Singers, Winchester Cathedral Choir, Music Projects conducted by Martin Neary in Winchester Cathedral on 21 March 1981. The cast was as follows: Donald Sweeney (Jesus), Brian Burrows (Pilate), Allan Mottram (Peter), Rosemary Hardy (Mary Magdalene), Penelope Walmsley-Clark (Second Mary), Linda Hirst (Third Mary). The producer was John Taylor, Bishop of Winchester.

The first performance of *Passion and Resurrection* was the subject of a BBC1 Everyman documentary: *The Challenge of the Passion*, shown on Easter Day 1982. The 75 minute programme followed the performance in rehearsal and ended with a shortened version of the *Passion* itself.

Full score and instrumental parts available for hire from the publishers

Duration: 90 minutes

CHARACTERS
in order of appearance

Priest

Jesus – baritone

Judas – baritone

Caiaphas – bass

Peter – bass

Annas – bass

Servant girl – soprano

Pilate – tenor

Procula (Pilate's Wife) – contralto

Procula's Maid – soprano

Thief – tenor

Good thief – bass

Mary Magdalene – soprano

Second Mary – soprano

Third Mary – soprano

Two angels – trebles

John – tenor

CHORUS divided into SOLDIERS – tenor and bass
PRIESTS – bass
ACCUSERS/ONLOOKERS - tenor and bass
WOMEN in the Resurrection garden - soprano and contralto

ORCHESTRA

Horn in F

Trumpet

Tenor trombone

Bass trombone

Tuba

Percussion (2 players)

Player 1:
Timpani, bass drum, small gong, 2 temple blocks, pair of large cymbals,
bronze sheet (or tam-tam if unavailable), tubular bells

Player 2:
Tam-tam, gong, snare drum, 2 bongos, roto-tom, vibraphone, set of crotales

Large organ

Chamber organ (ad lib.)

7 violins

1 viola

2 cellos

2 double basses

PERFORMANCE NOTES

In the event of a non-liturgical performance the work would start at Scene 1. It may end at the soloist's plainsong bar 1425, omitting the Priests's part and the audience Alleluias.

If in certain countries it is more appropriate, the original Latin texts, as found in the *Liber Usualis*, may be used for *Pange Lingua* and *Vexilla Regis* instead of the English. Indeed, any language which is familiar to the audience may be substituted.

SOURCES

The opening words are from the Church of England Book of Common Prayer, and the concluding versicles and responses are taken from the order for matins on the Holy and Great Sunday of Easter or Pashka of the Russian Orthodox Church. The concluding blessing is again from the Book of Common Prayer.

Scenes 1 to 11 are a translation by the Reverend Michael Wadsworth of an anonymous twelfth century Latin Passion Play from the Benedictine monastery of Montecassino.

The final scene (Resurrection) is translated by the same translator from the famous play-book of the monastery of St Benoit-sur-Loire at Fleury.

PROGRAMME NOTE

Reviving the practice of the beginning of Western drama, the two medieval Benedictine Latin church dramas I have used arise out of a liturgical event, in this case the Eucharist, with which the work begins and ends. 'Do this in remembrance of me'. The audience or congregation may participate in the singing of the plainsong hymns, *Sing My Soul*, and *The Royal Banners*, upon which the musical fabric is based, thus emphasising the ritualistic rather than the conventionally operatic nature of the work.

The eleven initial scenes move directly forward in austere, chant-like style: each character is accompanied by a musical halo more or less bright according to his sanctity. Instrumental interludes separate the scenes. Before the twelfth scene, which is concerned with the resurrection, the interlude idea becomes magnified to symphonic proportions as the crucifixion itself is acted out. The final, resurrection scene represents a musical blossoming of the previous style, where the inevitable and dire procession of events leading up to the crucifixion were depicted. Austere, dark, male-dominated music there, florid, bright, female-dominated music here. The instrumentation also reflects this division, with tuba, two trombones and two double basses (amongst others) on the one side, and trumpet, seven solo violins and viola on the other.

JH

Passion and Resurrection

JONATHAN HARVEY

a - bove ev - 'ry name.) Hear us, O Father, through Christ thy son our Lord;

through him accept our sacrifice of praise; And grant that these gifts of bread and wine may be unto

us his Bo - dy and Blood;— Who in the same night that he was betray'd took bread;

and when he had given thanks to thee, he brake it, and gave it to his di-sci - ples, say - ing:

JESUS
(off)

Take, eat, this is my Bo - dy which is giv'n for you. Do—— this in re - mem-brance of me.

PRIEST

Like - wise after supper he took the Cup; and when he had given thanks to thee he gave it

JESUS

to them say - ing: Drink ye all of this; for this is my Blood of the New—— Test - a - ment,

which is shed for you and for—— ma - ny for the re - mis - sion of—— sins.——

Do this as oft as ye shall drink it in re - mem - brance of me.——

Jesus

PRIEST *mp*

...in re - mem - brance of me.

CHORUS (some men) *pp*

...in re - mem - brance of me.

Off stage

4

SCENE 1: JUDAS AND CAIAPHAS

slower
30 JUDAS
Ha-sten the en-ter-prise. Sup - ply me ac-com-pli-ces, Hand-picked and stead-fast.

faster

Caiaphas
Take these sol-diers

INTERLUDE

36
JUDAS and the soldiers exit
Moderato

JESUS enters and prays.
With him are the disciples,
who settle down and fall asleep.

Caiaphas
Armed and   ea - ger.

Brass
Cb.
8

42
Vc.
(pizz.)
Brass
poco f

JESUS raises his hands in agonised prayer

48
Vc.
Brass
Vc.
Cb.
Org.
Cb.

52
Cb. pizz.
Vc.
Tbn.
Vc.
Tbn.
Tbn.
pizz.
Cb.

SCENE 2: JUDAS' BETRAYAL

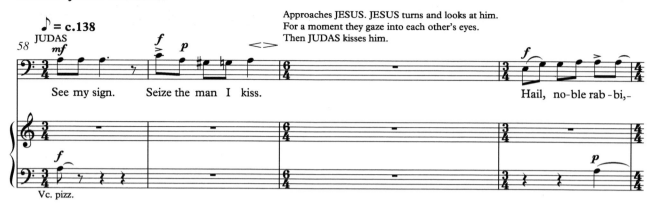

Approaches JESUS. JESUS turns and looks at him.
For a moment they gaze into each other's eyes.
Then JUDAS kisses him.

See my sign. Seize the man I kiss. Hail, no-ble rab-bi,-

Vc. pizz.

slower

— In whom No_ false-hood lin - gers.

Like a thief - tak-er Stealth-i - ly creep-ing, You

Str. harmonics (upper harmonics softer than lower ones)

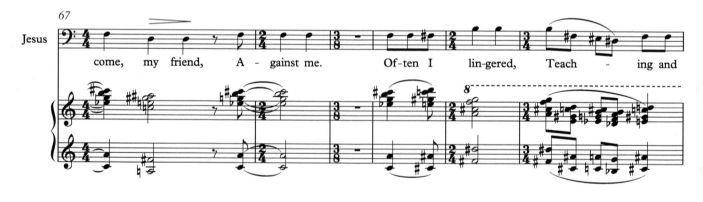

come, my friend, A - gainst me. Of-ten I lin-gered, Teach - ing and

talk - ing In street and Tem - ple. Then was the time to ar - rest me.

8

SCENE 3: PETER AND MALCHUS

SCENE 4: JESUS BEFORE CAIAPHAS

The SOLDIERS bring JESUS bound before the PRIESTS

12

allargando molto
Conductor motions
CONGREGATION to its feet

Pange Lingua, Part 1 (Mode iii)

CONGREGATION

All Sing, my tongue the glo - rious bat - tle, Sing__ the last the dread af - fray;__
Men Now the thir - ty years are end - ed, Which on earth he willed to see,__
All There the nails and spear he suf - fers, Vi - ne - gar and gall and reed;__

CONGREGATION

O'er the Cross the Vic - tor's tro - phy, Sound the high tri - um - phal lay,
Wil - ling - ly he meets his Pas - sion, Born to set his peo - ple free;__
There his sa - cred bo - dy pierc - èd Blood and wa - ter both pro - ceed:

CONGREGATION

How, the pains of death en - dur - ing, Earth's Re - deem - er won the day.
On the Cross the Lamb is lift - ed, There the sa - cri - fice to be.
Pre - cious flood, which all cre - a - tion From the stain of__ sin hath freed.

CONGREGATION sits
At end of last verse hold chord until complete silence has been re-established in the CONGREGATION

218

dim. a niente

14

SCENE 5: PETER'S DENIAL

SCENE 6: JUDAS' REPENTANCE

JUDAS casts the money on a table before CAIAPHAS

18

SCENE 7: JESUS BEFORE PILATE

The SOLDIERS bring JESUS, bound
and sagging at the knees, before PILATE

Pange Lingua, Part 2

CONGREGATION

All Faith-ful Cross a-bove all o-ther, One_ and on-ly no-ble Tree,_
(398) Bend, O lof-ty Tree thy bran-ches, Thy_ too ri-gid si-news bend;_
(399) Thou a-lone wast count-ed wor-thy This_ world's ran-some to sus-tain,_

CONGREGATION

None in fol-iage, none in blos-som, None in fruit thy peer may be;_
And a-while the stub-born hard-ness, Which thy birth be-stowed, sus-pend;_
That a ship-wrecked race for ev-er Might a port of re-fuge gain,_

CONGREGATION

Sweet the wood and sweet the i-ron, And thy load, most_ sweet is He.
And the limbs of heav'n's high Mon-arch Gent-ly on thine_ arms ex-tend.
With the sa-cred Blood a-noint-ed Of the Lamb for_ sin-ners slain.

CONGREGATION sits. Lights dim except for spot on PROCULA asleep.
At end of last verse hold chord until complete silence has been re-established in the congregation.

PROCULA'S DREAM

First apparition of evil

Second apparition of evil

PROCULA stirs . . .   . . . and awakens.   Summons MAID.

SCENE 8: DIALOGUE OF PROCULA'S MAID WITH PROCULA AND WITH PILATE

PROCULA

Ha-sten now, go To my hus-band. Tell him: Harm not This in-no-cent man, Mi-ra-cle work-er, Migh-ty

Procula

pro-phet. On his ac-count Ma-ny dreams Trou-ble me. This ve-ry night No rest I found. My

INTERLUDE

JESUS is released roughly from the column to be brought before PILATE

SCENE 9: JESUS BEFORE PILATE

Fairly slow

I mar-vel At your si-lence. No re-ply Es-capes your lips. Weight-y the char-ges.

They stretch out their hands against JESUS

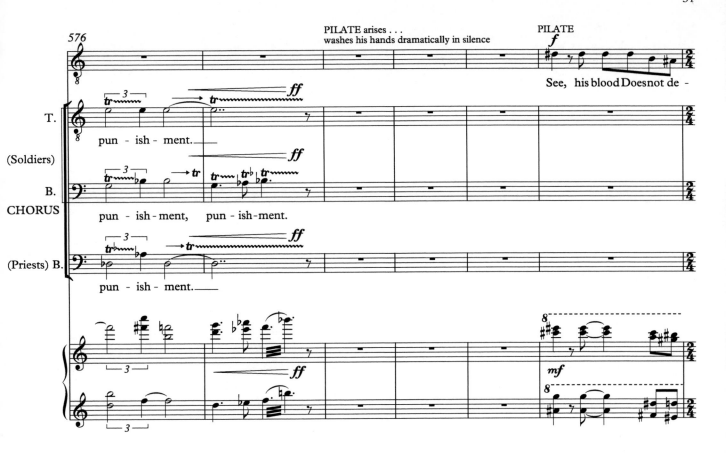

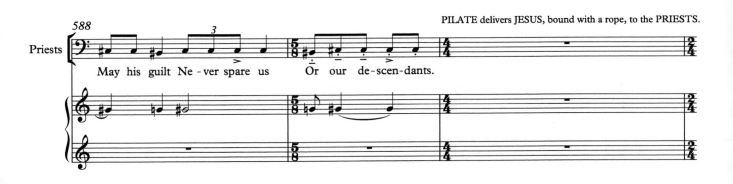

INTERLUDE

They lead JESUS to the Praetorium to strip him of his clothing

SCENE 10: JESUS IN THE PRAETORIUM

JESUS kneels at Calvary to pray

slower
JESUS

Fa-ther for - give them, for they know___ not___ what they do.

accel. - - - **a tempo**
(♩ = 66)

cresc. sempre

As JESUS is nailed onto the cross, the hammer blows may be heard in strict quaver rhythm, in groups of five or six.

(cresc.)

(cresc.)

The crucified JESUS is set in place, between the two thieves.

CONGREGATION stands.
Brilliant light on Cross
rit. - - - - - - **molto**

Vexilla Regis (Mode i)

754 CONGREGATION

The roy-al ban-ners for-ward go,— The Cross shines forth— in mys-tic— glow;—

(repeat chords as necessary to sustain harmony)

ff

CONGREGATION

Where he in flesh, our flesh—who made,— Our sen - tence bore,— our ran - som paid.—

2. There whilst he hung, his sacred side
    By soldier's spear was opened wide,
    To cleanse us in the precious flood
    Of water mingled with his blood.

3. Fulfilled is now what David told
    In true prophetic song of old,
    How God the heathen's King should be;
    For God is reigning from the Tree.

4. O Tree of glory, Tree most fair,
    Ordained those holy limbs to bear,
    How bright in purple robe it stood,
    The purple of a Saviour's blood!

5. Upon its arms, like balance true,
    He weighed the price for sinners due,
    The price which none but he could pay,
    And spoiled the spoiler of his prey.

6. To thee, eternal Three in One,
    Let homage meet by all be done:
    As by the Cross thou dost restore,
    So rule and guide us evermore.

[One or more verses may be omitted]

JESUS: Eloi, Eloi,
Lama sabachthani.

DEATH OF JESUS – Blackout

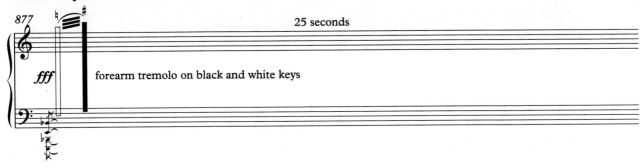

25 seconds

fff   forearm tremolo on black and white keys

DEPOSITION (dimly seen in 'blackout')

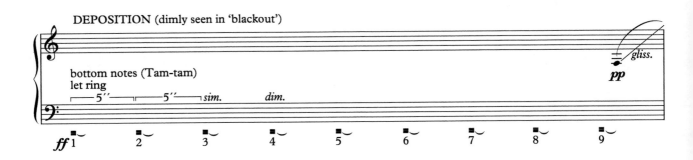

bottom notes (Tam-tam)
let ring

— 5″ — 5″ — *sim.*   *dim.*

ff 1   2   3   4   5   6   7   8   9

pp *gliss.*

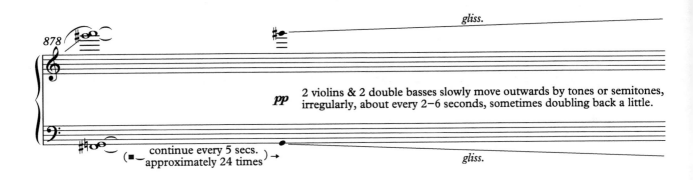

gliss.

pp 2 violins & 2 double basses slowly move outwards by tones or semitones, irregularly, about every 2–6 seconds, sometimes doubling back a little.

(■‿ continue every 5 secs.
approximately 24 times) →   *gliss.*

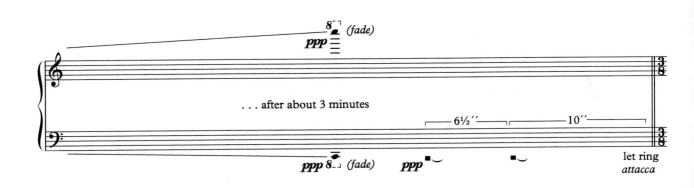

8‾ (fade)
ppp

. . . after about 3 minutes

— 6½″ — — 10″ —

ppp 8‾ (fade)   *ppp* ■‿   ■‿   let ring
attacca

46

SCENE 12: THE RESURRECTION GARDEN:
The three Marys enter in the dawning light, singing as they come.

An ANGEL appears at the door of the sepulchre, clothed in a golden garment, with a crown on his head, and a palm branch in his hand.

54

As PETER and JOHN go away, MARY MAGDALENE approaches the sepulchre.

entrance to the sepulchre.

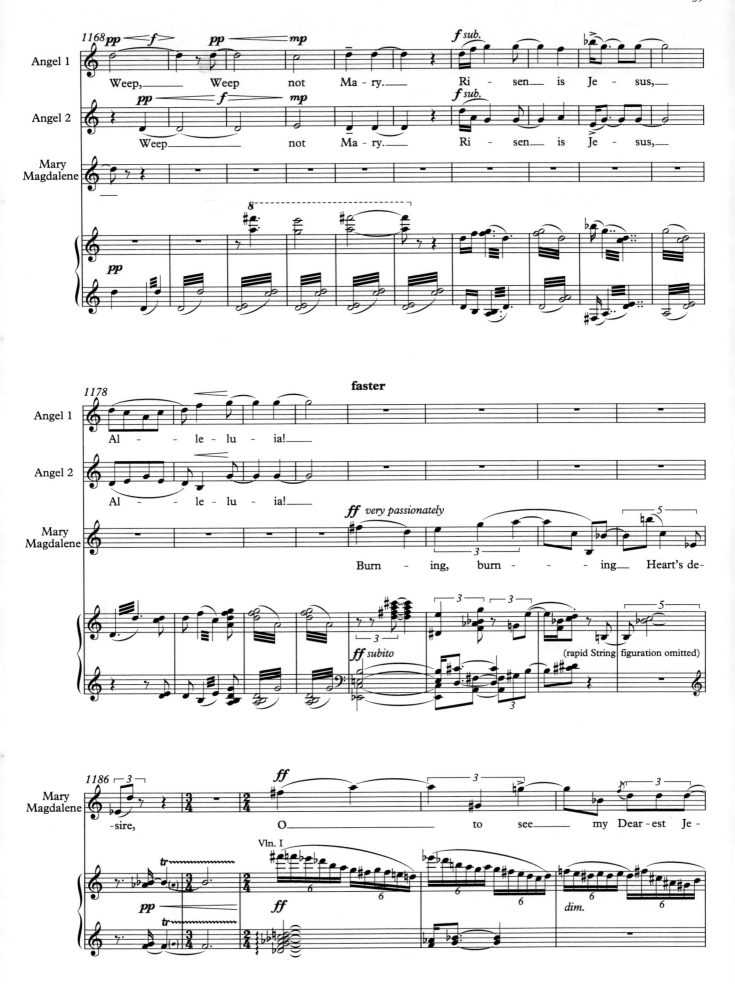

A man in appearance like a gardener stands near to the sepulchre.

1236

Jesus: I have not a-scend-ed To my fa-ther, Your fa-ther,

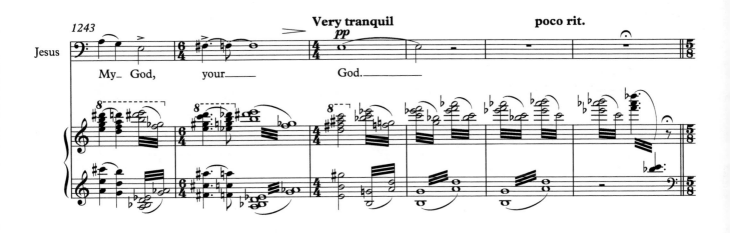

1243

Jesus: My God, your God.

Very tranquil *pp*

poco rit.

♪ = 176

MARY MAGDALENE

1249

Mary Magdalene: Re-joice with me To-ge-ther, Lo-vers of Je-sus. Seek-

1256

Mary Magdalene: -ing I found him, Weep-ing I saw him, Dear-est Lord Je-sus.

72

Kneel facing JESUS, who is high up at the back, so they sing *away* from the congregation.
Alternatively, they may disperse into the spaces of the church.

♪ = c.96 **Gentle but full tone, rubato**

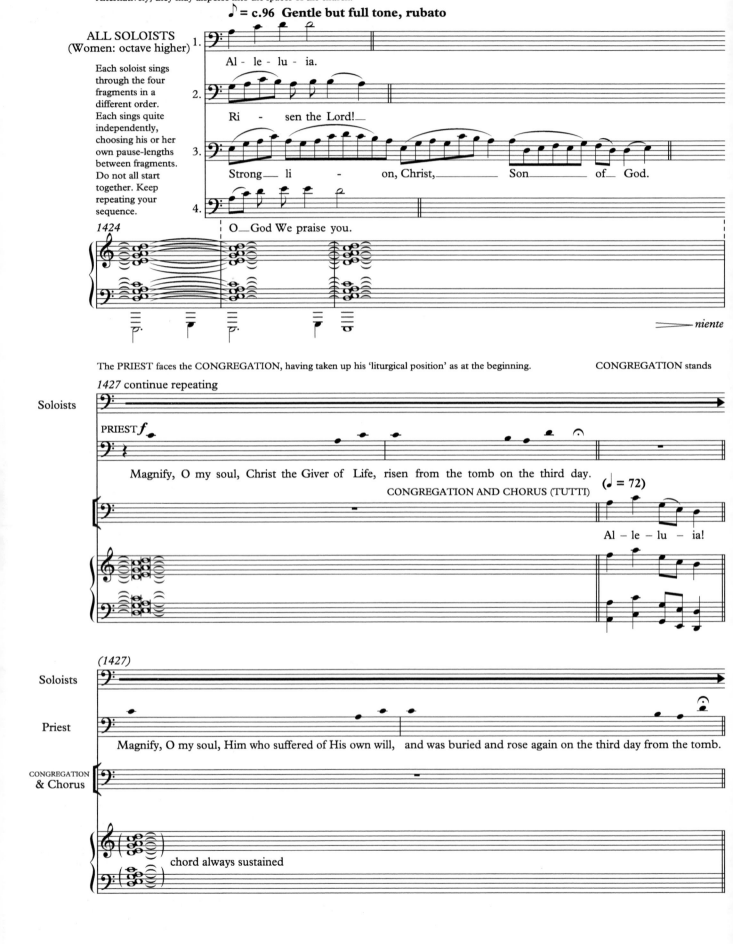

ALL SOLOISTS
(Women: octave higher)

Each soloist sings through the four fragments in a different order. Each sings quite independently, choosing his or her own pause-lengths between fragments. Do not all start together. Keep repeating your sequence.

1. Al - le - lu - ia.

2. Ri - sen the Lord!

3. Strong - li - on, Christ, Son of God.

4. O - God We praise you.

1424

niente

The PRIEST faces the CONGREGATION, having taken up his 'liturgical position' as at the beginning.   CONGREGATION stands

1427 continue repeating

Soloists

PRIEST *f*

Magnify, O my soul, Christ the Giver of Life, risen from the tomb on the third day.

CONGREGATION AND CHORUS (TUTTI)   (♩ = 72)

Al - le - lu - ia!

(1427)

Soloists

Priest

Magnify, O my soul, Him who suffered of His own will,   and was buried and rose again on the third day from the tomb.

CONGREGATION
& Chorus

chord always sustained

76

Soloists

Priest

In falling a - sleep, Thou hast awakened the dead from all the ages with a royal cry that roared like the Lion of Judah.

CONGREGATION & Chorus

Soloists

Priest

Mary Magdalene ran to the tomb, and seeing Christ, she questioned Him as though He were the gardener.

CONGREGATION & Chorus

Al-le-lu - ia!

Soloists

Priest

A shining Angel cried to the woman: Cease from weeping, for Christ is risen!

CONGREGATION & Chorus

Al - le - lu - ia!   Al - le - lu - ia!

78

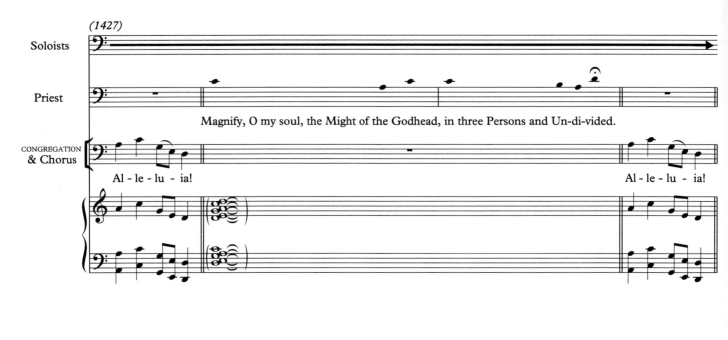

Magnify, O my soul, the Might of the Godhead, in three Persons and Un-di-vided.

Al - le - lu - ia! Al - le - lu - ia!

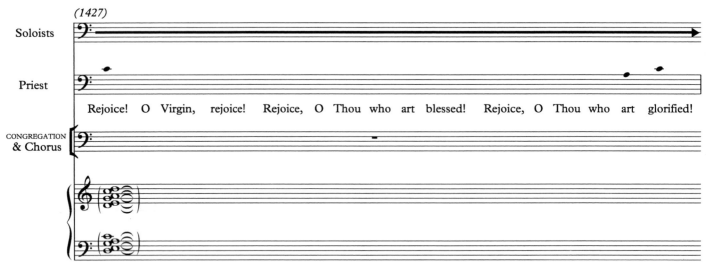

Rejoice! O Virgin, rejoice! Rejoice, O Thou who art blessed! Rejoice, O Thou who art glorified!

fade, finish off phrase *diminuendo*

For thy Son is risen on the third day from the tomb. The peace of God, which passeth all understanding,

Al - le - lu - ia!

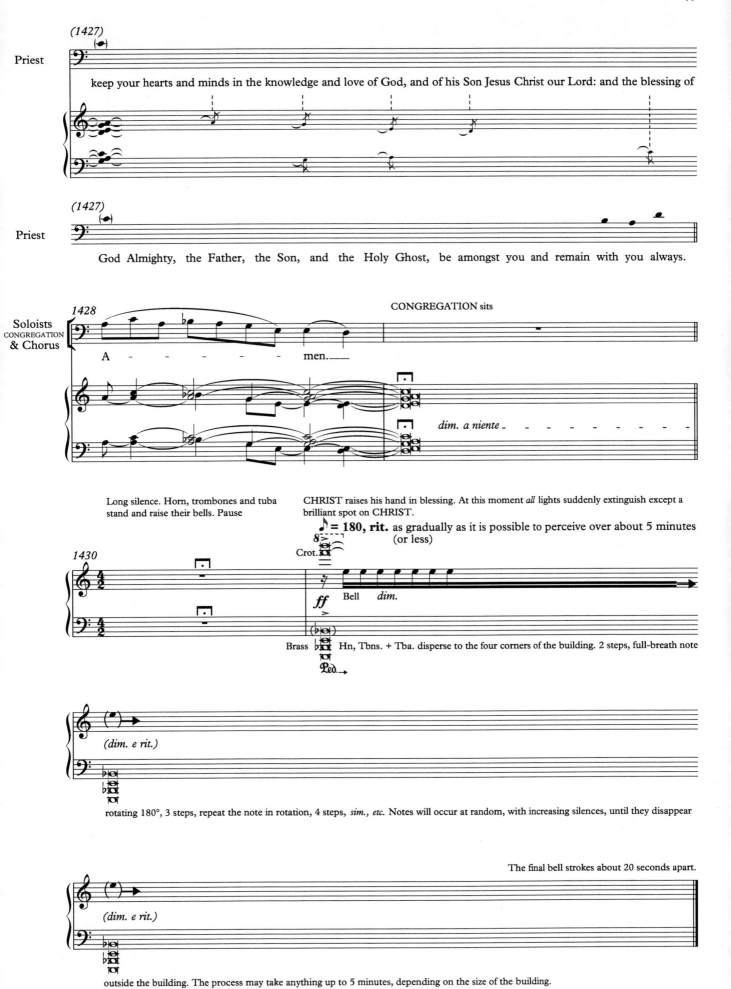

Priest

(1427)

keep your hearts and minds in the knowledge and love of God, and of his Son Jesus Christ our Lord: and the blessing of

Priest

(1427)

God Almighty, the Father, the Son, and the Holy Ghost, be amongst you and remain with you always.

Soloists
CONGREGATION
& Chorus

1428

A — — — — men.

CONGREGATION sits

dim. a niente _ _ _ _ _ _ _ _ _

Long silence. Horn, trombones and tuba
stand and raise their bells. Pause

CHRIST raises his hand in blessing. At this moment *all* lights suddenly extinguish except a
brilliant spot on CHRIST.

♪ = **180, rit.** as gradually as it is possible to perceive over about 5 minutes
(or less)

1430

Crot.

ff   Bell   dim.

Brass   Hn, Tbns. + Tba. disperse to the four corners of the building. 2 steps, full-breath note

Ped.→

(dim. e rit.)

rotating 180°, 3 steps, repeat the note in rotation, 4 steps, *sim., etc.* Notes will occur at random, with increasing silences, until they disappear

The final bell strokes about 20 seconds apart.

(dim. e rit.)

outside the building. The process may take anything up to 5 minutes, depending on the size of the building.